If It Helps You Sleep At Night

Chelsea Peseller

BookLeaf
Publishing

India | USA | UK

Presentation by *BookLeaf Publishing*

Web: www.bookleafpub.com

E-mail: info@bookleafpub.com

ISBN: 9789358735239

First edition 2023

To every person who broke me and didn't want be with someone who depression.

To myself for giving up on herself to now be coming back to re define herself

Good bye

Rose petals drifting down onto the pond.
I see your smile once,
Saturated petal; so similar to eachother.
Fingertips trace the water, your eyes glisten in
the dancing rays.
The water ripples and hums.
Spring scents fill the air, calming me.
The warm embrace of your arms, comfort thee.
The smells dismiss, just like you.
Now I'm left breathless.

Invisible illness does speak

I did tell you,
I told you when I was quiet all day.
When I didn't have the energy to even shower
for the whole week, because some reason it
seemed like just another thing to do on the list of
things to do!
I said it when I went to bed early and simply told
you "I was just exhausted!" The reality was I
really needed to lay there and let silent tears drip
down my face.
I made it visible by being present but not really
being there.
I told you with the mountains of clothes spewed
across the floor and the rooms always being left
a mess.
I made it known with the frown painted on my
face, no matter how hard I tried to smile or laugh
at the same old things.
I shouted it when everything I once loved, was
now something I couldn't bear.
I screamed it when the days just kept feeling
heavier and lonelier.
I showered it with the exhaustion in my voice.
I was saying it all when everything in my life
became so bleak.

I said it, I said it in every action, in the tone of
my voice, in everything.
You just weren't paying attention, you weren't
listening…. Just like everybody else.

Draining

I'm not so sure what's going on, except all the usual.
I can't lie tonight, I'm worn thin from it all.
I plaster a smile on as long as I can stand to.
Repeating to my reflection in the mirror, "I'm fine, I will be alright! No, really I'm fine." I continue saying this like a broken record, trying so hard to let the words help me get by. So much hope that someday these words ring true!
A scratch happens in the mix, quiet whispers flow back to me in a soft singing voice "you're not, oh how you're not!" It starts to scream.
"Please shut up!" Everything is silent, finally quiet as if I fell into a daydream.
The days are draining; I thought I was getting better.
Truth is, I'm only getting tired of this disaster.

Liar Love

When you lie are you the same person?
How many lies do you tell before they become
your truths in your own mind?
Your life is a rose stained color glasses in a fake
reality.
Must be so beautiful to see it the way you do.

Why do you lie? What does it do for you?
How'd you learn to lie so beautifully through
such crooked teeth?
Must taste like sweet nectarines.
I wouldn't know- I wouldn't know. I placed
those glasses on and decided to go along.
How many lies can one believe is true, before
they pick up the fate line between the truth?
I heard it over and over again; I guess I wanted
the fairy tale story you promised me.

When you lie are you the same person?
How many lies do you tell before they become
your truths in your own mind?
Your life is rose stained color glasses in a fake
reality.
Must be so beautiful to see it the way you do.

The sun rises and then falls.
Clouds form, then slowly drift away.
Moon goes through many fazes before it comes
full.
Stars are gas miles away from us lightening up
the sky like fireflies.
We could tell you all these realities but you are
so fixed on proving me wrong.
That's the kind of person you were and probably
still are.
I wouldn't know; I let it all go out the window
the moment you held hands with someone else.

When you lie are you the same person?
How many lies do you tell before they become
your truths in your own mind?
Your life is rose stained color glasses in a fake
reality.
Must be so beautiful to see it the way you do.

I hope reality strikes you like a tornado coming
down on a small town.
Oh is it still beautiful behind those glasses?
I took mine off the moment you left me stranded
with the brokenness inside my heart.
Tell me, are you the same person when you lie?
I think I fell in love with someone that didn't
know how beautiful he was just being his true
self.

Surrender

Breathing heavy and I can't seem to find way to
stop
Everything-everything is spinning out of control
1-2-3, 1-2-3, 1-2-3,
It's breaking under me, shaking and cracking
The ground isn't so steady; gravity is heavier
than a current as it drags me down... down...
down

Watching the darkness pull me in
I don't feel like fighting it this time again
I been doing that for way too long
So why can't I let it take me? Explain it please
I surrender- I surrender
I'm yours now, oh I'm yours now

Precious darkness come hold me
I known you from time and time again
Every time I think you are gone to find a new
friend
Here you are banging at my door, just begging
me to let you to come back in!
Now here I am; back to ground zero
Dragging, crawling through every day

Watching the darkness pull me in and I don't feel
like fighting it this time again
I been doing that for way too long
So why can't I let it take me? Explain it please
I surrender- I surrender
I'm yours now, oh I'm yours now

There is no rainbows or sunshine, so mundane
where I stand.
The clouds creeping into my head the sound of
thunder roaring in the back.
"Hello old mate, how have you been? I missed
us together, I thought you like to have some
quality time." Those smooth words with that
deceiving grin.
So charming, so beautiful and kind until you're
not!

Watching the darkness pull me in
I don't feel like fighting it this time again
I been doing that for way too long
So why can't I let it take me? Explain it please
I surrender- I surrender
I'm yours now, oh I'm yours now

I surrender- I surrender

Old Home

Sing me a lullaby with a catchy melody.
Take me back to our first night at my old house.
Wide awake as the night is growing late.
I want to sleep so deeply; remember the times
that made me grin and laugh.
Here and now, Butterfly wings dancing around
Beautiful colors floating in the night light.
Soft firefly kisses as they land on my hand
The soft glow going in and out like the soft heart
beat of a cooing baby.
Heavy eyelids start to come
Peaceful backyard sounds surround my ears.
The house is so beautiful and so relaxing to see
it all in one place.
The tree branches swaying, leaves rustling with
the sweet swooshing song.
The wind playing with my hair then before
going it pecks a sweet kiss behind my ear.
A dream ride to the moon and back.
The crickets chirping together
Reminding me how good it used to be.
"Hello old friend." The house says as I sit under
my favorite tree.
I push my feet off the ground letting the rocking
bench rock with the sweet summer air.

"Hello." I sing back as the dream plays on.
A leaf of red, orange and a tint of green gently covers my lap.
"I remember you and so much more." Cries the tree.
"Yes, tell me all about it." I swirl the leaf in my finger tips.
The lullaby is quite sincere tonight.

Merry Go Round

Giving me a minute to cool myself down
There you go again though
Slamming your phone down.
I will give you a minute and I will shut my
mouth now.
When the truth is the reason I am quiet is
because I'm shutting down from this constant
back and forth.
We can fight about it tomorrow.
I'm calling it a night.

Jump back on the merry go round
Jump back on the merry go round
We can keep going in, it's fun for a second until
it turns
Into the same old thing. I tried every horse and
every creature and seat.
Im kind of over it, how about you?
I will be in line at the roller coaster
Where all the other couples seem to get along
well even through the screams and downs.

I can't seem to get anywhere with you.
It's like having a conversation with the wall

And hoping Alice in wonderland and it will start
answering you.
Oh I am pretty worn thin of this
Have you noticed my exhaustion and how my
fighting gloves been hung up for awhile now
I fought long enough for the dream of a family
with you for longer than you would ever notice

Jump back on the merry go round
Jump back on the merry go round
We can keep going in, it's fun for a second until
it turns
Into the same old thing. I tried every horse and
every creature and seat.
I'm kind of over it, how about you?
I will be in line at the roller coaster
Where all the other couples seem to get along
well even through the screams and downs.

The view seems so beautiful when you are up so
high and it's just the two of you.
Looking back down from the mountain you
climbed together.
Screaming we made it and knowing even when
you go way back down together even for awhile,
there is another beautiful view waiting for you
two.
I guess unfortunately I have to do this alone.

I'm sure tears and heartache will come and go
like every day from the absent of you, but I will
get through…
Going to see the damn view even if it kills me to
do it alone.

Jump back on the merry go round
Jump back on the merry go round
We can keep going in, it's fun for a second until
it turns
Into the same old thing. I tried every horse and
every creature and seat.
Im kind of over it, how about you?
I will be in line at the roller coaster
Where all the other couples seem to get along
well even through the screams and downs.

I will be on the roller coaster waiting forever for
you.
Maybe our cabin seats will meet again, until
then I hope your ride with you know who has a
nice view too…

I'm getting off the merry go round today.

Heaven Forbid

If I let go of the idea of a heaven
Will I turn into a demon or simply become a
normal person?
It's sometimes cynical to try to be so perfect.
Half the problem is everyone believing in
something that isn't existent.
  We all keep on forgetting the biggest part of
believe is the lie hidden between the lines.
I pray and pray for the same things,
Do you even hear me? How do I know if you are
there?
People put so much stock in things they can't
even see or hear.
It's crazy and it's weird.
If you ever ask me the questions you be longing
for; we can sit down for hours.
I will spill the truths you been dying to hear.
A villain writing a love story.
Except who exactly is it here?
I can't seem to tell, cause honestly,
This time there is no hero that takes all the glory.
If this is the God you speak of writing it out ;
I think he needs to consider hanging it up,
putting it away for inventory.

Maybe plan better or have a better plan cause
I'm hating the things that been happening, my
man.
If I let go of the idea of hell,
Am I considered the devil as well?
Let's sit down and have a talk;
I have questions, so you have answers?
These unknowns feel like cancer.
I'm going to beg until I bleed dry
To know what to believe in when you can't even
spell believe without the word lie.
If I let go of the idea of heaven and hell, Where
does my soul lay when it's all said and done
when it's my time?

Thorns

Thorns come to kiss me.
So harsh the prick upon the fingertips.
Gasp while blood trickles down.
Red dancing so vibrantly, pretty.
It's the color of love and anger,
A beautiful color symbolizes two things together
Perhaps, just perhaps, I think…
That's why love is a complicated thing.

It's Late and That's It

We all go extinct once we are dead.
There is only one uniquely beautiful you.
You should cherish it and never let go of it.
Going numb, I'm dying inside.
Yet again, aren't we all?
They call me crazy, I say how much of it do you
want to see?
It's hard to love yourself when your demon is
laughing in your face.
Hate to love, love to hate.
If I can't walk next to you?
Can I walk behind? Admire all that's left of what
we once had.
Only in my deepest dreams,
in your darkest nightmares we aren't apart.
It's a strong current but it's the only thing that
makes me smile and frown at the same time.
You still live in my deepest dreams.
Visiting you each night before the memories of
you fade completely and I don't remember much
of anything.

Ladybug

My little ladybug,
How you love to explore throughout the day;
Then come home with all your findings in your
special jug; I love your ways.
My sweet little ladybug,
As big as you are today, I will cherish those
sweet-wonderful big hugs.
I watch you Growing stronger, wiser, and more
curious than ever.
I hope you never stop having that wonder, I hope
it lasts forever.
Imagination play with all your toys, asking
questions to help you learn about life and the
world.
My sweet ladybug,
The best twinkle toe dancer; my eyes sparkle
and my heart gleams watching you do your
twirls, whirls and special curls.
I know you won't be little forever,
So I'm doing my best to hold these small
moments so I don't forget, not ever.
Watching you grow up is so bitter sweet, my
prayers are that we always have a close bond
and never part.

One day you will see yourself in your own eyes,
if you could see you in mine, you never question
anything about yourself again.
Someday too soon, you will be your own little
woman.
Yes even so, when that someday comes and you
are 21
You will forever be my sweet ladybug,
That I will always look at and see, feel and smile
when I receive those bear snugs and hugs.
My sweet ladybug,
As unique and beautiful in everything just as a
quiet butterfly is.

Cupid

So is Cupid the stupid one or is it me?
Struck by an arrow and here I am falling for all
these asses.
Time keeps passing,
It's somewhat my own problem.
A hopeless romantic forcing love when it don't
want her.
Cupid, getting cold, my heart is starting to freeze
over, I feel a chill coming on, burr.
How many boys you going to send over?
Don't you see the time passing this girl by, I'm
only getting older.
I'm about to call it quits and dodge these arrows,
shoot and miss!
The last one never gave me a kiss good bye,
Still waiting on a happily never ever after from a
boy you sent my way named Chris.
Came to the closure, the last one was only a fake
bliss.
I will be like Barbie and my name will never
change.
Just incase though Cupid, if he misses me let
him know I haven't decided to flee.
I'm still waiting on a happy never after.
Hope Cupid gets its right sometime, or this time
my heart will be like glass and completely
shatter.

Octagon

How do I stop the demons from putting me in a
choke hold?
If I drown them in my imagination will that get
rid of them?
They might know how to float back to the
surface or breathe under water.
I haven't tried it, so you dare me? I love to, if I
knew it work.
They running laps after laps, dug so many holes
in me.
I tried it all to quiet them.
These drugs and pills ain't working.
The drinks are mixing;
I'm dripping to that dark place.
Rectangle trying to turn into a circle, while a
circle trying to be a square.
Funny shapes you turn yourself into just to fit in,
only to realize you truly never did.
I will be the octagon in the illusion.

Is There a Remedy?

If I write you a poem will you notice me again?
How about a whole damn novel with your name
plastered on?
Every page, even the title, there you are.
See it now, lining up, you made your scars.
Tell me, how do I get your damn attention?
I need to know cause I'm drowning here in this
heartache; I'm sure I did mention.
The loneliness is heavier than you would ever
know.
One half pressing down on the brake,
The half other pushing the accelerator.
Not sure which one to trust.

Fighting an angel and devil.
Doing my best to be gentle with this life.
I'm not sure what's right and what's wrong
anymore.
I don't want to be a bore, yet I'm following the
motions like everyone else.
Autopilot on and got nothing left to talk about.
Wake up and go, it's all a blur and I'm chasing
your mistakes down highway fifty seven.

I don't have many tears left in me.
Swollen up so deep in my soul,

I need some kind of remedy.
So much for getting high on cloud nine
Only to escape this distinct reality.
I promise I will be fine,
It's simply the practicality of my being.

Wake me up from my misery,
My mind is a mess rightfully a mystery.
I thought holding on would be okay but letting
go feels like a bitch.
I'm turning into someone I don't know,
Cast me an anchor or burn me like a witch.
I used to be best friends with myself
Now we are enemies no matter what length I
take to be back in touch.
Guess the writing is on the wall
It was good for so long, until that down fall.
No I can't remember when it happened
Only got these memories playing over and over.
Alone, alone, alone that's all I know
Not sure if I want to be sober.

I don't have many tears left in me.
Swollen up so deep in my soul,
I need some kind of remedy.
So much for getting high on cloud nine
Only to escape this distinct reality.
I promise I will be fine,
It's simply the practicality of my being.

Baggage Claim

Put that fake smile on
I'm losing my mind,
You will be okay, you will be alright
The darkness makes you so blind
It can't be as bad as the demons grind.
It's hard to be kind, when you're split in half and
zig zagged lines.

I got baggage, it's filled with fears.
If you want them, I will empty them under the
starlit sky.
Maybe it will make you smile knowing someone
bleeds just like you, or you will run and scream
like the rest.
Either way I'm here waiting like a mama bird in
her nest.

Why Do Good-byes Linger?

Now I have to remember you
Longer than I known you.
The memory always inside of me; it never goes
away.
Longing for you, this weird absent feeling still
some reason lingering.
It's the empty spaces in between my fingers.
The table for one at the diner.
Staring at the chair across for hours upon hours,
Until you forget to even order since the
conversations in your head got louder.
Everywhere I go, I'm reminded of the emptiness
you left beside me.
A concert without your voice singing out of
tune.
No more feuds, weird how I'm missing the
cockiness next to straight up being rude.
A bed with a big gap and a firm pillow because
your head hasn't laid upon it in years and years.
If I let go all together, I fear that will break me
and all I will have left is tears.
I want to remember as much as I can, while at
the same time wanting to completely forget.
Staring and talking to the walls once more; they
know I'm filled with so many regrets.

Butterfly Wings

A coffin for our love, I just haven't nailed it
shut.
Sometimes the most beautiful things in life
given, come from the ugliest realities.
I guess staying was the better alternative than
staying
Bleeding hope onto the picture; I stored them
away for the winter.
I didn't see it coming, so tear me to pieces.
Taking a deep breath, because I can't take the
heaviness plastered onto this existence.
I don't have much left to offer
You are all I have
So cut me open,
You can have the bare minimum of what's left of
me.
Here my darling, you can have my heart- my
heart.
Silent echos from the ghosts of my past.
If you loved me the way I am, you would have
helped me love my demons as I have loved
yours.
Now night time falls on me,
It's the tears that hold me under.

I keep on remembering that I need to be
forgetting.
Holding on tighter when I should be letting go of
this imaginary relations.
Butterfly wings burn,
Speaking to your soul on a deeper note, like a
whispering scream.
I hear you- I hear the apologies
I'm sorry I could never smile when there was
constant sun, but all I could see was rain.
Yelling monsters on the mountains
A loaded weapon right between the ears, always
ready to take action.
Blurry easy thoughts, mundane as these sick
games.
Do you want to play so we can get to fame?
Shut me down; I'm getting too old for saving.
So rip my halo off and shove me down below.
Cut me open, take me apart but please read the
note that states keep my heart.

Truth?

Too old to still be dreaming,
Buried those six feet under, it's too late now to
bring them all back to the surface.
I'm dying inside; I'm going numb.
Born a pessimistic somehow ended up with a
family of optimistic.
Hard to turn your brain around,
The world gifted me only knowing bitter- dark
and gloom.
Since the age four I saw thunder more than
rainbows.
I'm moving on and hitting fast forward.
Staring life down at age 31.
How did I end up here with nothing?
Praying to God for answers, to stop leading me
down a path of disaster.
So I get on me knees and I beg and plead,
Tell me anything but the truth at this point; I
don't really know if I can take the truth
anymore.
Tell me anything but the truth to my life,
I honestly can't figure out how I'm gonna make
it now
I said tell me lies lies lies
Make them as pretty a sunset

It's Hard to Love Someone with Depression

It's drowning in a tidal wave with an earthquake
shaking
A tornado is beginning
Eyelids so heavy but can't close my eyes.
Wake up early
Put the troubles aside
I need you to sweat it out
Run that mile without stopping, don't you pout.
You wanted this, you needed this,
Damn girl grab that heavy weight, let that sweat
race down your face.
Cry if you need to, let it all go, right here, right
now on this floor.
What's stopping you? That brain of yours? All
those voices saying no or you can't?
Get it out of here, this is for you, not them, now
go!
Heavier, harder, faster, this is the only way you
going to get stronger.
Consistency will come addicting like serotonin.
Routine won't feel like a bad program it will
come your lifestyle.
You got this, I promise.

Just let your troubles go for more than a second,
focus on something else for now.
A better version of yourself from yesterday, it
starts today.
How badly do you want it though?
It's go time, someday or is this your day one?

What's it like inside your head? He asked like a
melancholy song, as if that question is so easy.
My head? I questioned back as the thought
traveled in me. So hard trying to find the way to
tell someone what it's like to live with
something so uniquely shitty.
So I said…
The storm in my head is getting loud
The thunder and lightning clashing
I can't hear my thoughts as the rain starts
pouring
Pitter-patter, patter patter, drop drop drop….
Except it isn't as calming as it sounds.
It's loud and shattering; it's distributive and
destructive!
It's truly being stuck in a rainstorm in the middle
of a drive.
It hits out of nowhere and you have to just go
with it, ride it out.

The heart racing, the death grip around the steering wheel intensifies.

The pitter patter of rain hitting the car as you drive cautiously praying you are in the right lane.

The breathing stopping cause it feels some reason like you are under water.

The lungs filling up with air, your eyes water, the fear kicking in as the rain keeps pouring, it's not stopping no sign that it will!

Vision is compromised; it's dark and blurry, can't see much of anything.

Really can't tell where you are going, probably forgot too, all that one can think about is surviving this drive and nothing else.

That's what it's like to be inside my head I told him with a smirk.

He squeezed my hand politely and walked away silently.

"Was it something I said?" I thought as he left without even looking back.

Golden Cat

You are a golden cat
Meowing, meowing
The servants bowing down,
Too afraid to speak up to the crown.
You are a golden cat
I see you running this town,
God bless anyone who defends the rat.
Meowing, meowing to the top,
Letting the rest all back down and drop.
You are a golden cat
Praise you, obey you, absolutely adore you.
Oh my sir, my sir there you sat
So charming, such a brat.
You are a golden cat
Nothing less, but nothing more.
Too many fans that don't see you as a you are, a
real bore.
Meowing, meowing
When will any of them be done bowing?

Replay

Music is such a beautiful thing, it says
everything for everyone
when your own soul is heavy can't speak what
it's dealing with.
Let me be that for you; I want to be your lyrics
to your heart.
The sound track to your chapters and we don't
ever have to part.
Put me on replay, I got you covered.
I do anything to connect to you tonight and
forever.